Losing a Child

Text copyright © 1989 Elaine Storkey
Cover illustration copyright © 1999 David Salmon
This edition copyright © 1999 Lion Publishing

The author asserts the moral right
to be identified as the author of this work

Published by
Lion Publishing plc
Sandy Lane West, Oxford, England
www.lion-publishing.co.uk
ISBN 0 7459 4130 3

First edition 1989
10 9 8 7 6 5 4 3 2

A catalogue record for this book is available
from the British Library

Typeset in 12/13 Venetian 301
Printed and bound in Malta

Losing a Child

Finding a path through the pain

ELAINE STORKEY

A LION BOOK

Contents

The reality of loss

The house is silent.

There are no hungry wails for food, no sleepy chuckles of satisfaction after a good feed.

The bustle of childcare has ceased. The nappies lie folded in a sterile white pile on the dresser. The powder and the cream, the pins and the liners stand guard along the bathroom shelf.

There is no soothing rocking or cradling; there are no sobs of early teething.

The house is silent.

The curtains are pulled back, and light streams in through the bedroom window. The sun shines on the bright wallpaper, highlighting the mobile above the cot, which moves suddenly in the gentle breeze. It would be a lovely day for a walk, if there were someone to push in the buggy.

But the cot is empty.

The little familiar face that looked up to yours in trust and dependent love is missing.

Those chubby hands, expressive feet and funny little grins are all absent.

There is no longer any way of avoiding the reality.

That indescribably precious person is gone.

And all that is left is pain.

The uniqueness of loss

Losing a child happens in many different ways.

There is the loss in the womb.

There are cot deaths, accidents, epidemics, malignant diseases.

There are battered, neglected and tortured children.

We know how many children die a year. We know how most of them died. Statistics are published annually for us to look at and puzzle over.

But each statistic represents a real human life. A real person who, however young, had an individual identity.

And behind each loss there is grief. Sometimes it is grief mingled with guilt. Nearly always it is grief mingled with heartbreak.

Each lost child is precious. We feel each loss acutely, however we have suffered it.

We also feel each loss uniquely. Sometimes it seems as if no one else could ever fully understand our sorrow.

Statistics mean nothing. The grief is personal. The pain is mine.

The shock of loss

News that a child has died often comes with very little warning. Many children die as a result of accidents or through sudden illness.

The moment of shock replays endlessly in the parents' nightmares. They remember it for the rest of their lives.

It was like a blinding explosion in my head. I screamed. I wanted to shut the words out.

The whole world swam in front of me. I refused to believe it. I could make it not be true.

I wanted to rush past the policewoman to the little field where he always rode his bike. She was wrong. He wasn't in the accident. He would be there.

The world spins out of control. Something frightening and evil is happening. Other people seem to be part of a conspiracy – the policeman who comes with the news, the nurse who says all will be well, the doctor who offers a sedative.

The parents are in a dreamlike state. They find themselves going through rituals directed by other people. They don't really understand what is happening. Only two words have fully registered: the child's name, and 'dead'.

Even when the child's death is not unexpected, shock

is the parents' first response. Soon afterwards, questions crowd in.

Why did she die, and I survive?

How could he die first?

It doesn't make sense.

Parents who are in shock cannot be jerked out of it. Words, even kind words, are very often useless. Parents who have just lost a child cannot believe any words of hope. They do not want to hear them yet.

At this time the most help often comes from other bereaved parents.

They came and sat with us and said nothing for half an hour. We wept and they held us, weeping too and remembering their own grief. They told us that somehow, they didn't know how, we would survive the pain.

We would survive.

Loss in isolation

For some parents there is no public mourning, no funeral or flowers, no gathering of friends. A woman who has lost her baby through miscarriage may feel a very deep loss which few others seem to understand.

A woman I knew well was rushed to the hospital in her fourth month of pregnancy, bleeding heavily. The medical team tried hard, but they failed to save the baby.

The woman's partner was shocked and sad, but very grateful that her life was in no danger.

The doctor who called in on his rounds told her cheerfully, 'Don't worry, you've got plenty of time to try again.'

But, to the young woman, her miscarriage seemed like the end of the world.

She had loved that tiny child in her womb. She had developed a relationship with it. She had read books about its development. She knew its size and shape.

To her it was a real miniature person, not a lump of tissue. It was another human being growing inside her.

She was discharged from the hospital and received sympathy from family and friends at work. People told her to take it easy for a week or two. Friends ran errands for her. Soon she felt physically strong and looked good.

But deep inside she was in a state of frozen grief and mourning. She had lost her baby. Yet no ceremony had marked its death, and no friends had cried with her.

Similarly, those who have stillborn children receive no public recognition of their bereavement. For their loss too is seen, even by those in the delivery room, not as of a living child who has died, but as of a foetus that didn't quite make it.

The pain inside

I was with a mother whose son had died five months before. She was talking to acquaintances, replying calmly about her father's health, her daughter's school. When we were alone, I asked her directly what she was feeling now, how she was coping with her son's death. Her answer came very slowly:

'I've learned to smile in company. I've learned to appear calm and even relaxed. But this is not really me. It is a person that I watch going through the motions of living.

Inside, I'm still screaming, or else I'm just numb. Sometimes the ache is so strong that my whole body is racked with pain. No tablets take the pain away. They only dull my senses.

I suppose I'm just trying to hang on and get through life a day at a time. Sometimes I begin to feel better, but at other times…'

She fell silent, and her face looked tired and strained. We sat close together, waiting quietly until she was ready to go on.

'I woke up two nights ago with it all so fresh that he could have died five minutes before. The pain was almost too much to bear. I felt as if I just couldn't go on.

The only thing I could hope for was numbness.'

Why?

The pain and the questions are often bound up together.

Why was she born with an incurable illness?

Why did I have to miscarry again?

Why didn't I check that she was safe?

Why did he have to suffer when he couldn't even understand?

Why did the van come just at the moment she ran into the road?

Why didn't the hospital tell me what the risks were?

Why didn't he cry and wake us up?

Why did I let them out of my sight?

Why did I hurt my own child?

Why was she the one to fall off the rocks?

Why was it my son who was killed in the crossfire?

Why did the epidemic come to us?

Why did my child have to die?

The questions chase around inside our brain. We feel there ought to be answers. We feel we are owed some explanations.

Yet no explanations come, and there seems to be nowhere to go to find any.

Guilt and remorse

With the *whys* come the *if onlys*. Feelings of guilt are never far away. They can be very close at hand if we feel we are in some way responsible for our child's death.

Were we neglectful, too casual, too trusting, too impatient, not ready to listen?

Could we have taken away some of the suffering?

Could we have done anything more?

Perhaps we never really had the close relationship we wanted. Could we have shown our love more when our child was here?

If only I had been more gentle.

If only I had listened when she wanted to tell me something.

If only I had taken more time to do things with him.

If only I had bought him that little truck, given her that pet rabbit, done any of those special things that would have let my child know how much I cared.

Regret for the past is very understandable. It matters what we have done or not done. The *if onlys* can stay with us for a long time – even a lifetime.

Regret, guilt, fear, anxiety, and unanswerable questions. It is not surprising that a loss which affects us so deeply sometimes leaves us with permanent scars.

Children who mourn

When a child dies, family relationships alter dramatically.

There is now a permanent gap in the family.

Relationships with and between the other children change, and they have to be handled sensitively.

Children too need their own space to mourn.

It is difficult for parents to deal wisely with their mourning children. Grief can almost overwhelm the parents, and it can gravely affect the way they handle their children's sorrow.

A friend lost her little girl in a playground accident. The daughter and her brother had been playing together, and he had egged her on to climb to a height she couldn't manage. She fell and died of multiple injuries.

The mother was devastated, full of pent-up anger towards her son. For some weeks she was unable to forgive him. She confided to my colleague that she was struggling with resentment towards the boy. In her heart she wondered why he hadn't been the one to die rather than the little girl.

About six months after the accident, my colleague talked to the boy about his sister's death. At first he said nothing at all. Then suddenly he looked up, his face drawn and chiselled in misery, and said, 'I killed her.'

He knew his mother blamed him. He knew she had wished he had died instead of his sister. On top of his own deep loss, he continued to live with this guilt and rejection, even though his mother had long since stopped blaming him and had tried to draw closer to him.

Only after the boy and his mother talked it through together, forgave each other, and cried together was the boy able to go through his own period of mourning and begin to know peace.

Many children go through that kind of trauma after the death of a brother or sister. Losing this close childhood relationship can affect them for years to come.

Parents need all the help they can get. They often need to learn to built new relationships with their children. They often need to learn to channel their love for their dead child to those who are still alive.

Help from others

Yet it is hard to know where to turn for help.

Bereavement is a lonely experience. It is unique, and it is sometimes very private. It is often difficult to share our grief with another person, however close that person is.

Sometimes when a child dies, parents do not draw close to each other in their sorrow. Instead, after a time, that sorrow actually cuts them off from each other.

They may not know how to comfort each other. The words do not come easily, for they must first deal with their own grief.

Often other people don't know how to offer comfort. The tragedy of a young death envelops everyone in sadness.

Sometimes the wrong things are said. Well-meant words can hurt; observations intended to help can sound glib and superficial.

When we are grieving, we need time. We can't rush through bereavement and back to 'normal life'. For in one sense our lives will never be normal again.

A close bereavement is not something we 'get over' in the way that we recover from the flu or an ear infection. Instead the loss becomes part of us. We grow older with our memories, happy and sad, of the one who has died.

We need help with our grief. We need empathy and understanding. But most of all we need to know there are those who care. We need love.

What is love?

The capacity to love is one of the most wonderful things about being human. Love brings us much joy and elation. It can transform everyday routine into ecstasy.

Love helps us to make sacrifices for others, to live with inconvenience or hardship, to go the extra mile.

But love also leaves us open to hurt. It makes us suffer, grieve and ache when we lose someone close.

The pain of love has made some people regret that they are able to love at all. A writer once said he wished he were an automaton, because then he would never get hurt.

Why do we love so much, in spite of the hurts love is sure to bring?

Some people think love stems from our biology, as a self-preservation instinct. To them, love is necessary for our own survival and that of our offspring.

Others say love comes when people form societies. We contract to love and care for other people so that they in turn will love and care for us.

But love must be bigger than this. Many people love at great cost to themselves.

There is love that is poured out for others even when it is never returned. And love that leads to pain and death rather than self-preservation.

Why will a man dive in to save a drowning child at the cost of his own life?

Or a woman go without sleep for days while waiting for news of her missing husband?

Or a young surgeon risk contracting AIDS while working among diseased patients in Africa?

The question is real: Why do we love so much?

We love because we are designed to love. Love doesn't come from nowhere. It is not just a matter of chance. A loving God made us loving so that we will reflect him.

For love shows us that God exists, and it shows us what God is like.

Mourning together

One way love begins to heal us is through those who are close to us. We have been designed to be in relationship with others. We are meant to love our neighbours as ourselves and to show this love in practical and caring ways.

So the presence of old friends can be very important to us when we mourn the death of a child. We especially appreciate those friends who listen and look rather than bustle and talk; who just let us be ourselves; who are not embarrassed by sudden tears; who don't need to have things explained.

We are also grateful for friends who give practical help; disposing of things too painful to have around, answering the telephone, looking after the other children, giving us time on our own to talk through our grief, looking after precious photographs or toys until we can bear to look at them again.

We may find help in a support group of other bereaved parents, or we may benefit from talking with a counsellor.

The funeral is also an important source of healing.

It is a time when everyone together can concentrate on that child and on those who were especially close.

It is a time when everyone can mourn and comfort each other, experiencing the sorrow of the loss together.

It can be a public celebration of that young life, and it

can be a time to give the child back to the God who created it and loves it.

One father told me that at his child's funeral he suddenly felt completely at peace. He vividly understood that Bible passage, 'The Lord gives, and the Lord takes away. Blessed be the name of the Lord.'

Crying out in the dark

Two years after her son died, a friend was out shopping when she saw a tousle-haired child in a grey school uniform throw back his head and laugh in an uncannily familiar way.

Instantly she experienced recognition, hope and joy — only for those feelings to die away in fresh grief and pain. Without any warning she was engulfed again in memories that brought a flood of irrepressible tears.

It is not easy to come to terms with loss. Something deep within us resists it. We hang on to the possibility, however remote and unreal, that it was all a horrible nightmare. Soon we will awaken, and all will be well.

In certain stages of bereavement people often experience deeply satisfying dreams in which the child is back with them, the illness is cured and the wounds are healed.

These dreams can be comforting. They can give a waking sense of pleasure, of having been in touch.

But they can also produce an even deeper sense of loss, a greater longing to be out of the real world and into the dream world.

Comfort from others is often not enough. The only healer seems to be the one who has gone. But all the tears in the world cannot bring that one back.

Many people find prayer helps them in times of loss.

Still too stunned to share their feelings with other people, they can talk freely, without embarrassment, to God.

Some months after her daughter died, one mother spent an hour praying to God. She said that her time of prayer was like a memorial service, She was able to share with God all the little things about her daughter that she missed the most.

She relived, in her prayer, her daughter's shining face when she produced a perfect daffodil that she had grown herself for Mother's Day, the impish grin when she played a practical joke on her brother, the look of peace and calm when she lay asleep after a day of illness and pain.

The mother wept and poured out her sorrow to God, but she came away in peace. She was able to leave the child in a love and care even greater than her own.

Angry with God

Other people feel too angry to pray.

They are angry that God did not answer their prayers for healing or spare the pain of the child they loved. They believe he could have done so, but for some unfathomable reason chose not to.

An atheist asks how we can believe in a heavenly father, when he appears to care so much less than an earthly father. The earthly father does all he can to help his dying child, while the heavenly father seems to ignore all pleas for help.

Parents who once went to church to thank God for giving them a child may now reject God. They cannot accept that a God of love would ever have allowed them such pain.

Some parents feel abandoned and deeply disappointed. Their prayers have gone unanswered. God has let them down.

Others feel intense anger. Those who have trusted God with all their lives often feel this anger most acutely: anger with God's apparent indifference, anger that he allows such waste and such pain.

Even those who do not believe in God may feel anger towards him: anger that he doesn't exist, anger that at the heart of the universe there is only suffering and pain, not love.

One man told me how he wept and screamed in anger with God after his son died in spite of all his prayers for his recovery.

This is not shocking. Anger, bewilderment, dismay with God – these are normal reactions to death.

Even the Bible tells of good people's anger at God. Many of the Psalms express anger. The patient Job shouted at God, 'You are treating me cruelly, persecuting me as hard as you can.'

We too can be angry with God. He knows how we feel. He knows all our misery.

The danger comes when we are hurt but pretend we are not; when we feel deep bitterness and resentment, but decide to ignore it because we don't want anyone to know how much pain we feel.

The danger comes too when we feel guilty that we are so angry with God. We try to prevent God from knowing how we feel.

But there is no need to pretend, no need to try to hide our grief.

The experience of many parents is that when they do pour out their anger to God, they are released from much of their hurt. God then begins to bring healing, and comfort, and eventually peace.

On the edge of the world

People who have been bereaved are often left with a different sense of reality.

They are deeply changed by caring for a child to that very point where breath ceases and life leaves the precious body. Most are left with such mangled and tortured emotions that they have no words for them.

For some, there is a sense of relief. The child's suffering is now ended. The constant pain has gone for good. The life which would never have enjoyed adulthood is now released.

But there is also a sense of defeat. All our love, care and commitment wasn't enough. We gave our best, and it was inadequate. The child died in spite of everything we could do.

Those caring for children in hospitals can experience deep bereavement too. A nurse who had looked after a child for many months was devastated when he died. All the successes of her nursing career were suddenly unimportant. For here, death had won. Her experience was of utter depression.

Many parents experience something else too. They feel as if the world has closed off. They now seem to be living on the brink between two worlds – the old familiar world that now has so little to offer, and the new unknown world of death where the child has entered.

Some parents, in fact, lose interest in what they have been left behind with. Perhaps, for the first time, they feel ready to die themselves.

Closeness to death makes many people unusually aware of sights, sounds and smells. They may find the noise and bustle and harshness of our world hard to tolerate.

One mother told me she couldn't bear loud noises or bright lights after her daughter died. She preferred the gentle darkness, feeling that it somehow brought her closer to her child.

Losing a child often gives parents a new sense of the meaning of life. They realize that the world has its values wrong. Feeling incomplete, they long to be made whole.

For many people during that numbing period just after a child dies, eternity is much closer than life on earth.

A God who gives

The death of a child brings such a confusion of emotions. All the years roll together, with some memories standing out sharply.

We often remember too the birth of that child, and the experience of deep emotion that we knew then.

For even though the beginning and the end of life are very different, they are also similar.

They both bring that sense of being in the presence of something much greater than ourselves.

When a child is born, we are struck by the amazing intricacy of this new person: the softness of the skin, the minute thumbnails, the delicacy of that chin or nose.

Already there are facial characteristics, hand and leg movements and the ability to make very distinct and urgent sounds!

For the family, the experience is of having received a gift. We recognize immediately that this tiny being is not just a bit of its parents but is a person in its own right. In a real sense, it is an entirely new creation, and something which we have been given to love and care for.

The sense of 'given-ness' is something which we experience in many other ways too: the beautiful sunset, those magnificent mountains and hills, the powerful sea, the stillness and silence of an empty valley or a stretch of desert.

We are reminded of it also when we see a hidden, beautiful flower or hear a sudden tuneful bird call. There is that often overwhelming feeling that this has all been provided for us, but that we are not its owners.

Being surrounded by such gifts can make us reflect on who has given them to us. In fact we can know a lot about God just by looking at creation.

We see the order, the way all parts of creation depend on each other, the built-in healing processes.

We see the complexity, the amazing variety, the intricate details which are there in the structure of every eyeball, or every fingertip, or every leaf.

We see the uniqueness, the way in which, although there are millions of people in the world around us, we could pick out the face of our child or our friend in any crowd.

It is not difficult to believe in a God who loves us and gives us this wonderful creation. It is this God who makes each child unique, and so infinitely valuable.

But it is also this sense of uniqueness which makes the loss of our child so devastating and so complete. For there can be no replacement.

A God who knows us

Sometimes it is hard to think of a loving and giving God when a child has died. For many of those who weep, God seems distant, unreal, uninvolved.

But through their tears they are not seeing the whole picture.

In spite of our pain and sorrow, God is not distant and unreal. He is intimately concerned with all that goes on in his world. He dresses the poppy in its startling coat. He knows the very number of hairs on our heads.

Nothing is hidden from God. He knows us better than we know ourselves. He sees all our hurts and sufferings, understands us to the very depths of our being.

This is the God of the Bible.

What is more, the Bible pictures a God who is deeply involved in our suffering. This God is compassionate. He grieves with us, and he longs for our peace.

But if God knows all about our pain, why does he let it happen? If God runs the world, why does he allow children to die needlessly? Why do we have accidents, poverty and starvation?

If God really wants to give us good things, why didn't he make a world that was all good?

Why does God allow evil?

On one level no one can answer those questions.

All religions have tried to grapple with them, even

modern secular 'religions' such as humanism and Marxism. But no one has fully succeeded in explaining why evil exists.

On another level, however, the whole of the Christian faith is an answer to the problem of evil.

A tragic choice

The Bible says that God created a world that was all good. He created human beings to take care of this world and enjoy it. God's clear desire was that people would love his creation, love each other, and above all love him.

But love can only be given freely. We can't force someone to love us. Neither can we love for someone else. Love is something we give on our own behalf and of our own free choice.

So God gave human beings a choice. They were not programmed like computers. They could love God and follow his way. Or they could go their own way and live however they liked. Having choice is part of what being human is all about.

According to the Bible, humans did not choose God's way of love. Instead, they chose to go their own way. Their choice separated them from God. It separated them from each other. And it damaged everything in the world God had created. To use the language of the Bible, *sin* had now entered the world.

Of course, sin has not completely destroyed everything good. The earth is still beautiful. Human beings still love. But mixed in with the good are the results of evil.

Greed, hatred, wars, pollution, suffering and pain are now part of human life. And all of us, even tiny babies and small children, are now caught up in this suffering.

Evil is not just an alien force that attacks us. We cause evil too, year after year. We all contribute in some way to the wrong in the world. We add to the pool of evil whenever we hate someone, or act selfishly, or envy other people, or wound people with our words.

The things we do in our private lives are the same things that start wars in public life. Wrong is not only 'out there' or 'back then'. Often it is also 'in here' and 'now'.

When we lose someone we dearly love, our deep sorrow reminds us of the tragedy of living in a world where evil exists and suffering plays so great a part. In our sorrow we come face to face with evil. We feel it personally, and we often despair. It cuts us to the quick.

We wish we could cancel it out. We wish it had never happened. But, by ourselves, we can do nothing about it.

God's answer to evil

Since humans chose – and choose – to go their own way, it would be reasonable to expect God to wash his hands of the human race. In fact some people believe that is exactly what God has done: let us alone to stew in our own juice.

But, thankfully, there is an alternative way of seeing things. Christians believe that God confronted evil with love. Jesus, the Son of God, came into the world to live as a human being, to know pain and hardship, to face stresses and temptations.

The difference between Jesus and us is that he didn't give in. He lived life as it should be lived: close to God and full of love.

That is why Jesus' death is so significant.

On one level it was simply that the religious leaders didn't like his teaching, and the Roman leaders didn't like his politics, so they had him executed.

At another level it was that Jesus' loving life showed up the hypocrisy in other people, so they wanted to get rid of him.

But at the deepest level, Jesus died to right the wrong, to reverse the human choice for evil.

By dying, Jesus was paying for the evil in the world. He was making it possible for us to have peace with God. He was starting a chain of events that will one day end in a new world – a world with no pain, no death, no evil at all.

God understands how it feels to be bereaved, because death cut off the Father from the Son. In a way that none of us will fully experience, God knew deep suffering and separation and loss.

God's bereavement is the ultimate act of love. He suffered for us. And if he loves us enough to suffer *for* us, we can be sure he also suffers *with* us when death cuts us off from someone we love.

Feelings of guilt

At one time or another, almost everyone who loses a child feels guilty.

Sometimes the guilt is for real wrongdoing.

Week after week, a mother watched her boyfriend cruelly mistreat her four-year-old daughter. Even though she did not hurt her daughter herself, she did not stop the man from doing so.

Eventually, after a particularly violent beating, the mother became afraid for her little girl. After the man had gone out, she wrapped her in a warm blanket and took her to the hospital. But it was too late. The daughter had suffered irreversible brain damage. She never came home, but died some months later.

The woman said that it was only when the little girl was admitted to the hospital that she came to her senses and realized what she had done. She then understood that she had played as much a part in her daughter's death as the man who had beaten her. Every day she awakened to the memory of what she had allowed.

Sometimes, however, people feel guilty because they have imposed superhuman standards on themselves.

A mother put her five-month-old daughter, who was snuffling with a cold, down after her feed. The mother was extremely tired. It had been a very heavy day with a baby and a toddler, and she was not feeling well herself.

During the night she heard the baby cry. She meant to get up to feed her. But in her exhaustion she went back to sleep as soon as the crying stopped.

She slept soundly through the rest of the night and woke up the next morning feeling well and refreshed, surprised at how late it was. She soon learned why. The baby was dead.

It had happened during the early hours. At the inquest the coroner made an observation with complete disregard for the anguish of the parents. He said that if the baby had been lifted during the night and the mucus in the lungs had been cleared, she probably would not have died.

On a rational level, the mother knew she was not to blame. Emotionally, her sense of guilt remained.

Two mothers with a deep sense of guilt. How can they – and we – come to terms with it? For each of us it may be different. Yet at one level it is the same.

We all need to be put in touch with God, who can forgive us, assure us of our own worth, and enable us to forgive ourselves.

God alone can take away both real guilt and the sense of guilt.

Facing up to ourselves

One of the most difficult things for people to do is to admit they are wrong.

We are afraid of losing face or being criticized. It's easier to blame others, especially since we can usually find good reason why it's their fault.

Admitting we are wrong so often gives other people an unfair advantage over us. It also means there is something to put right.

But if we don't admit we are wrong, we can't accept forgiveness. It also becomes difficult to forgive others. In fact, we often end up locked into situations where no one gives way and there is never any reconciliation or healing.

Even when we long to make a clean breast of things, we often don't know how. Sometimes we are overcome and obsessed with guilt. We feel we can't get rid of it, no matter how hard we try.

These problems are common in many situations. But they are especially real after the death of a child: not necessarily spoken about, but eating away inside.

Forgiveness

Forgiveness is at the very heart of the Christian message.

It is what Good Friday and Easter are all about.

When Jesus died on the cross, he was not simply being unjustly executed by a Roman state. He was willingly dying for us.

He was dying so that we could be forgiven for choosing to go our way, not his.

He was dying so that our guilt could be removed.

He was dying so that all the results of sin – accidents, illness and even death – could be destroyed and we could get back what we have lost.

On Good Friday Jesus experienced torture and darkness for us, so that we can now have peace with God.

On Easter Sunday Jesus rose from the grave, so that we can have new life with him.

What does this really mean?

It means we can face up to the wrong things we do and be released from their hold on us.

It means we can be forgiven for all the ways we have let other people, and ourselves, down.

It means we can be healed from the effects of turning our backs on God's way for our lives and going our own way.

It means we can completely forgive ourselves, because God knows the truth about every situation and forgives us completely.

It means we can dare to lose face, to admit where we are wrong, and to ask for forgiveness – because that is exactly what we get. Forgiveness, love and restoration are now possible.

There is no guilt too big or too small for Jesus to take away from us.

Those old memories that still hurt – speaking roughly to our child, not being on time at the school gate, breaking promises, not listening – can be healed. Where there was real sin, it can be taken away,

We simply have to ask forgiveness and mean it, to pour all our sorrow out of our system, and believe in faith that Jesus, who died in our place, is alive and offers us forgiveness and friendship.

Where there is guilt and remorse, forgiveness is the beginning of healing. And where there is forgiveness, there is life and hope and love.

A wasted life?

Many parents feel bewildered, not only that they have survived their child, but that all the potential locked up in that lovely young person has gone to waste.

The world has certainly been deprived of tremendous talents because of young deaths – music, art, scientific advances. Prospective thinkers, political leaders, writers, dramatists, engineers have all died before their time.

People who would have made wonderful parents, spouses, friends and neighbours have for ever been lost.

When parents have glimpsed in their young child's unfolding life all that might be possible, it is not surprising that at its untimely end they cry, 'What a waste!'

But we don't know enough to be able to say that. We don't see the world from God's viewpoint.

Only God knows just what that child has already contributed. Only God knows just how much has been accomplished by that young life, even when it was full of pain and sickness.

Each of us contributes far more to our world than we could ever understand or measure. Each life, however short, plays an important part in God's plan for the universe.

When we can grasp this and give thanks for it, then we are beginning to heal.

Letting go

The grief that was so acute and painful in the early stages of bereavement grows into a permanent sense of loss as the months and years pass.

Life goes on. New routines develop; new opportunities open up. But for some parents, feeling freedom from grief even temporarily can bring new sets of problems.

One mother found she could no longer picture her son's face with the same clarity as when he had died.

She had always been able to concentrate and bring back every detail of his skin, his muscles, the shape of his nose and forehead. Suddenly she was aware that, although she could still describe what he looked like, she couldn't see him.

For her this brought an emotional crisis and a new sense of being left.

Some parents feel distressed when their other children are able to laugh loudly only days or weeks after the death. They do not realize that children cannot sustain grief as constantly and unbrokenly as adults.

For some parents, their own ability to laugh again does not bring relief. They may refuse to allow themselves to laugh, feeling that laughter would betray their dead child. They feel they must hold on to their grief — even though it is painful and draining — because, if they do not, they will lose their child again. For the child, though dead, is brought close through grief, and losing even this closeness would be unbearable.

Yet the child is no closer or further away whether we laugh or cry. Parents who have let go of grief, knowing it will never fully let them go, find they never forget, never cease to miss the dead child. But they slowly begin to survive life without the child.

Letting go is not betrayal. The love between parent and child will never disappear.

Hope for the grieving

When we are grieving, we can feel such a confusion of emotions that our minds and bodies become exhausted. It can seem that there is no relief from the depth of pain that engulfs us.

The Christian message speaks hope to those who despair.

It says we can be forgiven for all the wrongs we have done, and we can have peace with God because of Jesus.

It says death is not the end of life, but just part of the journey, a milestone we must all pass.

And standing right in front of death is Jesus, who says, 'I am the resurrection and the life; the one who believes in me will live, even though he dies.'

For in his resurrection Jesus showed us that there is life after death, and a life without pain.

But for our suffering now the Christian message does not offer us easy solutions. It says rather the very reverse: that this world is hard and life can be very difficult.

The sin in the world has brought tragedy and misery along with it. We are all affected by this; we all live and die with it.

Even God is affected by the world's sin. He chose to suffer the anguish of bereavement in order to bring hope to us.

A relationship with Jesus helps us begin the process of healing.

It brings us the experience of forgiving and being forgiven.

It brings us the knowledge that we are ultimately safe from all harm, because God is in control and nothing can separate us from his love.

But it will not take all the pain away. Jesus himself did not escape suffering.

It will not answer all our questions. God alone knows the reasons for our loss.

Yet it will put us in touch with one who can share our grief and carry our sorrows.

It can help us understand that at the very heart of the universe there is not despair but hope, not evil but a God of love.

A word of encouragement

From a letter of Paul to the early Christian believers at Rome:

> *I am convinced that neither death nor life,*
> *neither angels nor demons,*
> *neither the present nor the future,*
> *nor any powers,*
> *neither height nor depth,*
> *nor anything else in all creation*
> *will be able to separate us from the love of God*
> *that is in Christ Jesus our Lord.*